OF SIRENS, BODY & FAULTLINES

OF SIRENS, BODY & FAULTLINES
NAT RAHA

BOILER HOUSE PRESS

THE MARRIAGE OF GEORGE OSBORNE
  & IAIN DUNCAN SMITH (EPITHALAMION)

[OF SIRENS / BODY & FAULTLINES]

£/€XTINCTIONS

DE/COMPOSITIONS

my teacher says there are more walls in england than in berlin, johnny.
what were we to do in those crumbling acres... ?
— *The Last of England*, Derek Jarman

RADIO / THREAT

to vladimir mayakovsky, 12.54am

       objectivities :
                    enclosures momentary, the reproduction
     of quietude plugged
                      to relief, contingent.
                      telegraphics historical to this homestead
now dazed off emissions, the daily
                        grounded upon wreckage
                        of common relationals drives
shipwrights from surface, spontaneity, "friendship as a way of life".
              union fails you to bullet.
              beneath concrete & glass...
                             the logic upon my
              lover fetishises her beauty, leaves.

     to break the capital's substance / doctrine of bliss & suffocation
     indexed by ring & other, we might wake in peace.
              tomorrow the continuation of raids, the price of bread
              & whisky, etc.;
                      wornout in the circulating hours

(late letter, waterloo bridge 11.31am)

       concern fraying eyes of us
               occupying
     abstract ,
         hectors to bleep vicious tones
         of the day / repetitive circular /
wet sourced to heads / pulling various our bodies
                  , to city
                 where you
    dressed favourite , labour the good without remuneration.
      worn less verbose / shackled by the
      should of the hour's disciplinarity / kid's scream / fearing the
moment closed enroute by
       statutory glass, capital's monument //
that I steal this for health,
       from theft of whatever self might
  be here given lips to beam / possibility tangible as the
  bulldozers creep turf graffiti / accumulate /
     to not share the site of breakfast
              of sorrow humming quiet, umbrella
     cheaply exchanged.
           to act
   from the poem, might nurture the
   retained
      between our
          distribute permanence & surplus, between
  the slipping & constants that dry muscles exhaustive
transformed as pageant-daily
        / despondent week public-I & its fiction;
        you exit not knowing the clock.

take treat out of day's mediocrate :
the bmp of our clothes
interact down / thin vague of energetics to
gauge of residential
internet mediate / dangles barest strip of your
known speech && throw
locate sickness stable
by vibrations
of floorboards reflects the
cheek-direct, it is the
coldest year in the city
/ subject-disparity masked the apparition of social belonging
& days lacking beauty of anyone / wanted to
drain my monologue / hours
in peace of subjectivity evol'd
from dissonant body
/ nomad trauma / partial-hang in subcultures, known
imperative / bring 'morrows

intensity-siren connect street to corneas / timescale
imbedded , beside the
glare vicious of fun peoples /

tense /
in wh   we

drench / worn less verbose through
procurement of rest w/ owned hours:
embedded; spring cut to look quiescent by
neo-beauty / of political necessity:
to shred exclusions in relationals logic
/ tangible under duress
/ shield eyes from mem. / shield graze of audio

(lunch poem)

coursing thought hum lunch hour to
orange swoon of
                    your cut the
                    pleasure memory in public ,
               'cross room tories smirk to laptops
                                  celebratory apparent
  dull june meteorological
                        ground qualitative
                              under shell rabid material hate / in want
             to give kiss to soothe the overwork
                                 stiff to musculature / limbs
                               my / to wrap to your /
                             cognitives strained
           hours lacked restful in the cusp of pleasure feeding back to pour
           joy into what we
                   sell for declining real terms,,,
                   reciprocate the hold of beauty 14:09 received
  as the room grey hung light fills
                        business quietly it is the day after I
                  sold my birthday droning clatter of formalised
                  speech *being here well negated*
                            the styles of
                  women for the dayworld & suits
                    turn/re-
                         investment serves dayspace
       [breathe]
                  draw back embodiment ribs
                          to smile, your qualitative
  through the text as I flag nerves
                    & so on repetitive strain another
             image from police raid at 40 Beak Street in Soho, London
             #stopg8 pic.t******.com/RumrW2neM4 9:44 a.m. how
             real are our slogans today how real terms the wage
             how sigh have to do job apps today /
                       induct the self here

wish the curve

        arm comfort public lights off

            the big society network at the meeting table form
            welcoming gestures "yes good / basically we
            // intellectual, creativity, athletic in the areas our
            communities & schools" sic before tax//
reproduction formal culminate ableist economic:
            bodies divergent

                    cut from the knowing

[poem. in absolute solidarity the southall black sisters demonstration against the ukba, 24.10.13]

smiles electronics for the border
                                force great walls of dover,
                                heathrow & stansted, tax animate
            xenophobe in the
                                private security form / detention
theresa may neocolonial marionette,

                                apourosity of borders for labour / blood
                                phantasm that the human denied to follow / the
                                regulation of the senses as collateral to capital
                                deregulation, the administration : illegal
                                mobilisations against 'illegal' bodies, perpetual
                                dream realised in kettled touch, the common
                                in action ukba –which has been abolished–
                                                & golden dawn / bombed out
                                HQ / vomit national front sloganeering / *tell*
                                them you do not want to talk to / no
                                answers a wall of resistance necessities of
                                contemporary everydays / scab
                                reports new asian family in street [1986 *cf.*]
                // landlords of soho &
        peckham , absent birdsong by traffic smog AM
        new cross road , alarm/ing peace / walworth
        feelings on the street today ⌐ the
        heirs of london & windsor, the people's
        republic of south london, district insurrections
        & dreams / to which we might migrate——

            cf. crumbled wage half-life / experimental employment, standards
            of living instants taking selves -blank- 'cross waterloo
            westminster bridges & home, arms giving in rooms inefficient
            in poems written as labour theft / the
            being of government, consciousness &
                                will financial,

8

borders closure raised trafficking, the will of
human subjects global attempts at survival
social determinates / *imf wuz here* / the emptying intellectual
blinkered facing appearance justifying the austere,, & i
homewards from supermarket / sustenance seek the
helicopter looking up bourgeois st. new cross a dog
dragging teeth out of a black 'suspect'

                                          arm spurred by met dozen
monday PM we
                 listen to the property screaming & you
are outside the jean charles de menzies memorial, stockwell &
texting sad
                 & I hear the face of david cameron he is a two-tone
house alarm it is autumn & warm the seasons deranged, the names of
future bourgeoisie, the cries & calming of royal children,
steps in a capital tourism to derelict / modern rot,
                          source-funds 'art
                                    means business solutions'
                              the years since artists thought/had
                                    to burn down the city //

galore in staying wake trill soft us

upon each suggest

to consider in pleasure

≠ before you/i draw sensate / quiet

streams to skin composed

&& arms around to dress ,,

pressing tangent/ temples & cheek\bone

\degrees 120 across neck in kiss:::y/our/s

sweet to musculature paths across\

that we invent passion here

in critique of universalisms,,,

that the labour to keep selves in

challenge of particulars our divergent bodies experience,,,

that to give hands // lips public to each

gains the signifier lesbian & politics is not a given,,,

that our genders socially contingent

& evolving in critique of the same,,,

that *inflammatory homosexual* is bracer rouse necessary

of desires we work to externalise from relational our;;

designation to us slipping enunciate relation adjective

accrued social form as image particular;

whereas *dyke bi punk riot drone sonics* does not

circulate the wealth does not on mainstations we

speak in thrills relative ## by

flesh temperate for arms softkiss before

timepolitik construes AM upon plural

that we will be tired in hours free from our wage work /

left to domestics

,, you holding & close \ shoulder to

button print resist psychic death

(police dream)

day's cuffs / saturate content of subcognate, *just*
a dream in my ~~[#]~~

                police formations replaced prime hour cultural
                aliens /television saturday, to clampline neoliberal apparatus
                sections our demo forms :: the opposition of anti-fascists
                denoted clear in hours of ~~our~~

                              document / fixed electronic
                              south east border towns /
                              debit cards & private ability
                              assessments --
our potentials in the
                language of totalitarian computers,
domestics precarious in the undercut, ukba
enforcement in lewisham, billboards & cinematic
imperialism / abnegation
                of male faces in the smug wet
/ petal of the shard workday 7.11P.M. spectral officer formations
of night hours wails fixed into & from our throats ~~[#]~~ secure
underground stations & canteens, strip vitality sonics
saturated city space protest w/ capital fuzz investment, the
english defence against tower hamlets, dead radio signals
news channels, negating state violence / class & migrant
history, the pale arms of
                rupert murdoch / rhetoric identical outstretched
                evening silent drains of custody blood, deskilled
                contemplative possibilities in common words
                abandoned flags of royalist / ketamine, multi-brand
                made in britain / ready-to-wear exports kettles
                nerve gas, the great fires of brixton & tottenham, the
                police kidnapped at cable st / investment capital theft
                , reversals of the everyday ~~[#]~~ dispersal bailed
                winter since 1979 //
                      ~~[#]~~ action absolute now

wealth harmonics / ˜ / negative series

::: 'british' jobs mythology, a history of
global blood & appropriation; consider
who now severing the workmind /
feasting economic / funds public
handed corporate ; the

unemployed reserve mutated to latent 'workers' shocks
frantic & starvation quote "looking for
yr future potential state productive
equates = £70pw 'wage' (sic) 'free'

jubilant dictates morality
[insert su   deployed typical ref. business practice
iain duncan messiah weekly that
vulnerability will force 'productive'

descen(job cathedral / birdsweet
by echo of sirens, wage lie, lie food bank
cavorts lie jcp vulture hoard ╪ bomb fetish ;; or
deported, the value & investment in
/ migrant hate tory pr salaries
&/or tabloid editors the

£figure that can be transformed into social fear
operating against the recognition of agency
& material need *cf.* acts of insolent british
citizenry / that the

increase of migrant workers necessarily
sources profit accumulation it is the

2015 general election {#} QUESTION 16: the words
'britain', 'british isles' or 'british', however, are used
in this test to refer to everyone in A)
england B) the corporation's city of london C)
serco yarl's wood detention centre
D) policeofficer at door [S]

= spectral theresa may
[insert surveillance] the
lyric you of television ╪ you &/or
descendents of empire windrush passengers,
cavorts to democratic violence

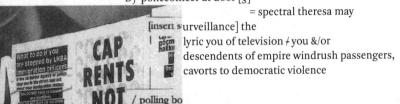

/ polling bo

                    in pronouncements of inverse
                    oth myth absolute
                = financiers queuing to enter parliament radio
                4 air dead of eastern economies & difference
                / all economies are negative histories bodies
                        & lived exploitation relative
                        to the word 'fair' in all mouths
[s] impossible beliefs of liberalism here
in the 21st century when we do not exist &/or suffer

the modern legal system is not for saving you
in absolute solidarity with CeCe McDonald

        limit for static
                change in assignment,
                registered to throes of bureaucracy: that
protected characteristics
                cf. status quo conservational
                society inc., mythologies
                where privilege of a/recognisable common sex is
                    unrecognised as privilege,
                                  whose being
                does legislation represent?

        whose disclosure to
                        the bounds
        white classed liberalism,
            the false grails of the free in ties
            & employment, beside the colour of the
                same in employment
        difference slated to 'the same as but',
        with fear or something---; reproducing
        the scene of happily //-til she
            blood cut a fascist with her labour tools,
        state oriented against intervention, of the necessity
        to exist still in the AM,// 'cept the sanction
                              of good / of
socially-necessary incarceration/ dear
CeCe speak / feeling beside the *'can'*
/ not by list of our
                trans* collective global loss / break
                the pillars / amnesiac ⫻
                burying the ribbon & its referents
                ⫻ deviance struck off the // official
                history of civil rights according us freed –
                compelled through the prohibitions

[july 2013]

made a promise for a ¬ commodity excess / infatuate
antimonies salvate
                    institute in dabble health / poetics
    / contemplative
                    bureau-rational transformed into the every
                    day in our trying to sell labours /
art negative to public life / industrial creativity / buyer first time
                    percentage debt allocation,

                                        service of dead publics aggressive
                    mugs closest, my ¬ inverted pleasantries english
                    take / good will */victim out of/* extracted from concept / *"we*
                    apologise for the / theft of hours prior / *made a*
                    victim stretched through sad / resentful to & fro by
                    train to families / priced against
                            possible pleasure take / sediment hurt yours
                            fractures the looking calm forward
                                            service taken to taunt / stress
                                            / debilitate weeks
                    ♮ invisible domains of price felt by increase in sweat
                    / anxiety fret chemical downtrod *victim* self
                    perfect rational of simplicity / *due to today's busy*
                    individual / & *you feel you can*
                                        drained vitals & the arms &
                                        mind left to give / to others our
                    kisses from the foot of workplace , pre-
                    exchanged for wage / ~~my working~~ sensory trauma in the
                    need of service *induced manipulate* ,, feeling relational to the
                    opacity of produce / comprehension at the fetish dam *where*
                    the future's not ¬ withdrawn out of the palm, for / profit
                    vindicates the necessary, the possible dull
                    strange infatuate in the high st, burnt coffee
                    chain visuals ¬ shark service self-exchanged ¬ wallet
                    overdraw,, in use to reach the social &/or
                    subsistence struck through secrete misery, what / emerge to
                    hour / object's material hit hectic on present toward self-
                    distain nerves fret to life in
                            normal missed on inact false false
                            advance zero privatised hurt hit the ¬

~~##~~ *your* value indication from
experienced poor *high street*
bank crime ripping
the private austere *your personal*
national debt fragment / gorged
derivatives ~~##~~ here in
london SE *this / atm will soon*

        permanently out of service 27th
        september 2013 your nearby / "spectral
        objectivity" / contained in false
        standard / *"calling local bank to keep*
        appendage to a desire of growth

autoproclaim [::] will endowed in *the shard is a*

, its child glass
/ familial construct blood ozone

-illuminate

sold fictive autoproclaim
[::] contemporary beauty of speculation << monumental
makes me / lie to my friends>>
conception block [doused

casts of dirt / object-identitytype
weighing every london rooftop stench

aspiration / national foul in
commercial/domestic claim to dwelling transformed post-LAPSO §144

⫝̸

from transport
<static *street* overseas *corp power / on*>
internal mutations / washed cross lines of
our flesh & lungs struggle / steroid clear , kept
hooked inflate & scars / to care in kiss *cf.*
:: the
number of times
you have been told to think not ::
duration saturating being
perspective daily / landscape
"engage, disrupt & deter" life &
sleep by pavements humanity &
increasing through thameswind
neglible-net-worth *cf.* numb persons
ALL NEWSPRINT IS MYTHOLOGY

AUTOPROCLAIM [::]

the shard is peaks PM_{10} particulates
upper thames / millbank dressing glass
thursday / marquis of granby SE14 NO_x
92 µG/m3 ⌞ $PM_{2.5}$ 89 µg/m³ ⌞ PM_{10}
107 µG/m³; for turning to sickness
; logo of urban landscape ⸬
; overaccumulation ⫽

; stunt ray skyscraped to fixed capital street assault / image perfect
that our words crossing subject realise publicity value our
squeals coexisting across work/labour distinction hyperstatic object-i exhaust

    shard freedom to speculate / social
    demolition / rebuilt honour / south asian blood
    untranslated to dirham to pound
    circulates *to the heart of*
    >>*lie to my friends*
    sun hung freeze hands of personified
    >>*street with the white financial* kidnap bankers
  that the wharf parasitic eyeshot / line nook
  nightby old kent rd / that our local mutates
    ≠ mutates new trains mutates w/ popular
    haunts / commercial tucked bourg. urban
    transplant valley hollar outdoor untitled
    ex-shopfront that they started to superbia / hit
    mechanical history / started to
    ~~[#]~~ supermarket // that *your estate agent* / 2nd in
    peckham, which belongs to none of us,
    that they rack us by our leased shacks ~~&&~~
    season of crisis produced over human

THE MARRIAGE OF GEORGE
OSBORNE & IAIN DUNCAN-SMITH
(EPITHALAMION)

George Osborne, god of love, we have spurned beauty –
— Sean Bonney

conservative love = the absolute colonisation
of the social senses.
political sedation
bestows the being-subject onto partial us,
impelled stakeholders. queer life privatised
in a moment of
subcultural needs / surplus on the
back of affective provision, where our
qualitative use of the marriage-form
is legitimate only
through its exchange-yield;
where our possible love is depoliticised
as multicultural inclusivity girded from
bone capital/
where LG(bt__) is a series of summerskills linear
w/ new norms i.e. acronym sold to close down
content / we extrapolated to financed change
that negates us / bodies known through markings for
happiness-as-refugee in the fetish trait,
between the vow-thing & the
happily ever consumed ;
there is no talk
of fucking here.
the marriage-form
weds economic selfhood
freshly denies racial / gendered
/ sexual / disabled / unemployed abject,
negated from perspectives as scrounger–
i.e. get married or get deported;
the crowd taught to only sight normal/other:
the congregation is a pride parading to social
conformity
/ g.a.p.-ad happily sold not to stitch
/ comprehensively spent regulate / the cruelty
corporate
liberal gay optimism inflicts on under-subjects
/ the happy coupleformal neoliberated
through active material hate;
no compare to material inequality, 1/4

homeless youths still queer, of trans* subjects
sutured to disclosure in the name of right:
our gendered beingness extra-legal, of the
strictured possibility within administered
thought & the felt / boundary
stray to political lockout / insufficient investment /
capital-legit sociality negates the necessary of divergence.

GEORGE: lo! the wishèd day is come: we
announce the latest action to secure recovery;
that shall pinkwash the gays to usury of long delight:
that we value marriage *socially* and *financially* &
doe ye to usury of joy & privatised sexual pleasure sing,
on the back of material cleansing to which all
must answer with all its social consequences, & its
ring that I give to you, Iain, as a symbol of my love,
choosing to bestow austerity with you.

all gays with garlands goodly well, buy
this union
as image, public-corporate for my fayre love,
of wealth and endless things

& goodly *all* agree with sweet consent, to this
commodity celebration of coupled norm. hark!
how the cheerful gays chant of marriage's praise,
their recuperation in this world, fundamentally fair

fair Austerity! shew forth thy vicious ray
and let thy lifull heat fervent be,
for burning the scrounger beings &
welfare state, with fresh lusty-hed, go
to the bowre of my belovèd love; we enforce
on our public three principles: growth, reform
and sick fairness– ascending british enterprise
& economic culture it needs
to win the global
race in honour of capitalism; making sure we
are all in it together;

26

now is my unending love all ready forth to come
in unbroken circulation: let this day, like all,
be myne; let all the rest bequeathed to you, Capital;

    the which the base affections doe obey,
    and yìeld their services unto your will;
    once seene your celestial, unrevealèd pleasures,
    wrought by your own hand, then *all*
    do wonder, and its praises sing:
    spread thy broad wing over my love and me,
    and in thy sable mantle us enwrap,
    from fear of crises let no dread disquiet once
    annoy the safety of our privilege; pour

    your blessing on us plenteously, & your
    happy influence upon us reign–
    that we may raise a large surplus
    through the earth that you do long purchase
    saturated with market-grown happiness

DAVID CAMERON: bless O Capital, that
Iain and George bequeath, may they ever
abide in thy transformations, together
in privileged unity, love, and happiness, amen.

GEORGE: Iain, conjunct to all desirèd lending, I
join our lives to this economic plan, of a
downsized state, minor democratic, of private needs
material, emotional, political, to be
its partner in life. to honour you &
not let the poor leech upon us through their sickness
& in health, nor other undeserving subjects:
migrants with their mischievous, numerous childs
they shall pay £3000 to enter our empire;
NOR the disabled, whose need we sense not;
let no lamenting queers, nor the dolefull jobless,
pour foule horror on the pleasures that thee, Capital,
wrought, honest and faithful they must turn up
with a CV and look for work & only after the seventh
day shall they receive the minimum amount of money

    the law requires for life;
& the number of persons working for our public, esp.
women & northern folk, shall fall
by 144,000 in our next years of happiness & health

& we are to remove automatic pay rises simply
for time served to this public & these
are consequences of public investment; & those
who do not utter thoughts in our language must speak
it or we shall not pay them.

        plebs! go to your wonted labours this day
is expensive; we plague thee
    with the greatest unfairness
    & we dub this progressive government
        w/ the pledge to plague thee today,
        tomorrow, and always.

IAIN: & George! my love, of applecheeks which the
banks hath corroded, I promise to join my life to your
counter-terrorism budget, that we may cut Muslims
from our biggest society, & having severed the equality
& human rights commission budget by 76% our love shall
grow sustainable enterprise through others' sickness
and in health, especially the disabled
who shall be reformed back to work through common
personal independence payments & quantitative outsourced
health checks which shall eliminate tens of thousands of
pounds/persons; & we shall universalise them
& the underserving poor to workfair for 30hrs pittance,
& end all legal aid to the austere crises'd ordinary subject
whose demolished life quality will forever be

                their responsibility
& cut £11.5bn from our public's tax purse that
        shall disporportionately free the ourselves
        & the richest, who have already purchased
on credit the marriage commodity here
in the city of westminster, its 20 year ad campaign:
abject parody / commodity-form equality, a fused
community of enforced economic interests
rightfully into which
        all homos may crawl, beauty bestowed
from democracy corp., through these difficult times of
happiness and sorrow, all the rest of their lives.

        GEORGE: my right honourable love
arysing forth to run their mighty race, clad all in white
some angell Iain had beene. he has

comprehensively won the national debate about
welfare, his balding head alike melted tight
currency, vacant eyes debase the poor, countenance
enraged that they

                thieve his handouts, fayre man
garnisht w/ privilege's beauty! glorious w/ corporate love!
now available as rights-based sacrosanct
ceremonies that it may produce & sell

                          such endless matrimony
DAVID: why blush ye, ministerial loves, at its exchange-value
      give to me

            your hand in its pledge
            never had men more joy then this///

  in newsprint *defenders of marriage say the darnest things,* yet
  their fantasies are negatively realised as our
    impoverished everyday. NO PARTIES. NO PEACE.
    QUEERS: PRIDE IS NOT OURS. ORGANISE.
    FIGHT BACK. ACT UP.
        SCREW NEOLIBERATION:
        START A REVOLUTION.

[june 2013]

[of sirens / body & faultlines]

((a fire))

fractal history in the cut of flames.   stateorgan
                brick 'lapsing / context of materials
                geography particular.
                                bones damp / emotive solidarity
                        for the rare thaw of sun, the sight
                        capital fixed through smog our lookout 100m+;
    even the scrawl
                abolished social support still marking the firestation
                                                    , bound
            / your mind & /
            ankles to anxious
            when it takes me
            out days the i
            -chained.   stalked
                            & skyscraped by
                        monuments of finance.

            present history ::
                        for our secondariness is out for us
                        to turn eyes too,
                                transgression particular
                            [[samples of feeling in tunes lost
                                        unwritten /
            unremembered as a simple class of identicals:
            constraint #̶ *sketching practices to collectivise herstories,*
                        negating the self negative in the owned ; the
                        absolute need to self-determination
            of lives & our culture, as the work of decolonisation
            && for new manners to
            smash fascists,, anti-semities
            backing the dead of history./ the
                        city in the summertime

                                                                33

good morning

war has arrived
here the twenty first century //
sovereign, democratic]]   worn to absence / structured
                                                    labour sleepminutes
                              / we,
                        her majesty's;
                  we, classed liberal subjects; we,
                        white feminists; we gays identical
                              trapped by the
                              fetishism

        charge of the gentry.
        scenes of pollutant song & short
                                        eyes, concentrations
                              increasing white bodies dispersed
                              early hours, new cross road:
                where we've held out in the try collective of us
                to construct a wedge stable , of permanence. we
                              so broken out of belonging together
        , root & rubble piling upon action to bruise, to be
                        thrown only back into privacy
                                                    / landlord behest::
                        sick w/ increase on values, the
                        suffering of our friends
                                        / this exact their
                                        dream of estates, contemporary
                                        good life / magazine pleasure
                ""all profit is identical to exploitation

                ` `\\defences 'gainst the transformations: speculative
                values, wage distributions / vague opportunes,
                news orchestrating semblance of growth. the
                        false universal
                                              ,
                              „— faultline our concepts of home,

early restrained 'cross the head to

wear

/ to give care & joy
to you under thatcherite architecture

,, bliss of contemporary
draining the nerve / when

we will need to hold, extremities
of feeling,/stress of
inaction / hierarchy of the land
onto ~~us // & we,~~

~~with residence~~

, affection & sense exact
to conditions of the age & market &
fear newsfray / / entertains mind
/ mode to takeout night hours. if
communication w/

their world conditions
of days,, sever;
stable toxicity ones zeros minutes caffeine
drained.
to just for / rest in the ends
& be w/ selves [:] disintergrate
workplace projections the
/ infinite astral
counterhistories:

the condition of the workforce 6.21pm; 11
.08am job centre of violence eminent. state
to save tensions &
dress of fears
to secure through grey in the daily, transports
etc. that this always more partial –
than the supposed / givenmodes life ;; that
fret draining from eyes from back musculate
& limbs ** each hour

being,, encouraged
out of our memory
officiated & shaking hands w/ reward :
as thefuture days free from the wage
decline w/ the wage itself// art effacing

blocks demolition that house the we
repeated from invisibility, the experts of collision
& coverage

autumn in august corp.
infatuating on the health
of us / the value of sickness, the
plasma of friends in youths;

neocon bridging into dreamstates perspire
& try to // nerve rest extracted behind eyes.

reactionary fiscal
action to
erase rebellions of youth,
to move from dispossession is to not be free,
to chain in exploitation the
production of security, food;;

break this basis / volume kind
repairing heads that bare daily
/ that we must enable our
possible action / that every government
on the globe will fail again this today / install
fear on prey finance, the
bourgeoisie chased from brixton village.
how for militancy to half such pleasureseeking
the decline in quantities sustenance afforded
// predictions of survival
/ to terrify the circulation of pounds

the future according to urban capital
vapourfear phone tap threaded
, keeps the sovereign entertain
-ed /secure
& the movement of papers

of future hunger & workhouses
of persons overdosed on the
everyday;   *good morning, racist toxicity*
          time disintegrate reading the newsprint *cf.*
          that thought on the justice of your life ˧ freedom as
                          privilege reflect/delivered
                    in the law's tongue ,, if the
policy ⚊(bodystate contained to standardised
requirements /descend into hell /camberwell 20.14
hrs ;   *the news is our daily bread, gives us momentum*
                    , provides orientation,
                    sensation personified
     persecution˧ poverty, torture : contemporary imperialist accord
of human rights / finance aspirational to
     have never dreamt the fence, guantanamo
     the negation that keeps the democracy clean.

[august 2014]

before stretch tide momentary clasped to waking / curl
of arms kind unclothed on side slight curve

                          shouldering downward your line
takes breath moment ‹ * › defeats italian futurism / h. moore-ish more homo-flex
as your waist tucks to round

               the hip, postures struck our crook
               & noted pull intimate ⌐ * *
               limbs ,, conscious of the worn fibre

      / musculature below
      / ribcage on both
     // sides , thorax trialled months prior to the

                          swell of company, ;

    /// difference pertains to physicality

                   ⌐ beside medical shifts & wears;

              constellate all of the above
   && the cut of you :: relational
    & mind & curls & action
  & the A.M before the worked day here south of the city ;
relative
      to the line yours to claim breath,, i offer self to cup

                    attach crux of evenings , wear

                                        &
                            breath looping
                                        of the
                            felt backwards // continuous,
queer love as radical praxis
& the simplicity of fox hats.

                            roads quieter

                                        , as if for
                            cleared demolition; falling
                            out of referents & to remain by
                            south east co-ordinates // as all
                            voters, commuters
                    , struggle on cognate, fingers with to show

                                        & condemn,
        the freeze encroach & apartments wind up &&
        idealism, persons asleep fallen homewards following
            day limits of orbit H spinning light, the
                            gravitation clutches at desire :: positions
                        spun stalling new stigma & television
                identical abjecting the

                                    arms & waists of us as there &
                        in parent's eyes –– vacancy / social
                    violence falsifying all plurals

                        . what I of held through
                        poems / grain love

                                    universal & the DWP
                        & the chill home from wagespace
                                    & BU12 AGV unmarked re-
                                    versing onto amersham vale

(poem announcing the end of england)

on the occasion of sick order & separation
, papers
rabid w/ future according to corp.:
stultified peoples known as the english
, epidemics of national conservatism
, freetrade publics &
service / borders wretched keep
calm & ~~carry~~ ←colonial ghost ;;
our sickness , downriver sold & quantified to
the TTIP. in 2015 \
with all ships &
symbols of order
charred, vendettas of the middle
ages, tearing the
brick / reign barricades
westminster, of monuments demolished,
speech signatures & corpse tories, fascists
& centrist tendencies: we /
to hail the end of official history. in waking
/ destruct semblance of the democratic,
the extractions from our bones pronounced as the new week, positive
witness \ stupor & individual interest,
home owned & other aspirations//
a comedy of damnation
AUTOPROCLAIM [:] & erasure of the countryside

:: we none will be saved by weathering & climate's end

[september 2014]

>> street with the white financial kidnap bankers

                    second split
of all fireworks looping / saturate
entire sky compliment w/ every
                              siren bright to
                              point of tearing all ears &
                              eyes enlightenment
                    . you turned to thank
offering , obscured constitution
of minds, bloods, limbs charred
                              , an image for digital
                              friends / rats myth as equal
                    owners ground rivers knee-skimmed viral
                    mutated official hygiene brand
                              now they took your name & flagged , so
                              happy in the minor distribution
                              of warmth \\ season abolished the soil
                                   abolished, radiation-free ocean abolished,
                                        economic democracy
beautiful in yur passport headshot entry in
                              paleness destin-
                              ations of vitality / descent the
                              traffic according to theresa
                              may *'cut by*
                                        drowning at sea'
k-hole politik to point of sharing where
all essential intention & contradiction
are outside the click of understanding,
                              glam ancient react to grow
                              up in progress & happy keep
                              the global south enchained

(shoes, danube)

placing out the ankle, still

pɛʃt sight widening
such of history upon the limbs of you
/ teetering i
out of spectators consciousness

all liquid erasure   second unreal glazed to heart that
clocks, economies of empire   the poem weak to catch
/ colour negative truth   cinematic
&
freeze near
tears
before we know who, where
yous were taken from .

love : necessity : anti-fa :
& the value of all boots here 1944 - '14
- prehistory / our stomachs
curl w/ relay televisual rocket another
palestinian house collapsed, continued
the long twentieth century

,, my eyeslide & accumulate /
laid 'cross generations we are
retelling to days of us, arms as

bronze & you 35mm holding vac a case
wrapped quiet / 'til we
instigate politics

echo out immediate universe
/ its frail coherences. grasped
against poverty
for preservation / memory ground out

abolition
accumulation of future wealth,

, churning
emotives :: what we can
gain in space & archive /#
amnesiac quotidian & demolition
[july 2014 / march 2015]

                    pulled from
ease ⟨⟨ slumber
red in eyes &
                rubbish of workdreams, new
cross road sirens unmarked, GEO vans & sun
-flowers
            smogthroat waft, the years less
desperate only through the replacement of people
            class glean slight on
            53% salary toward at home / begun
            / felt in our sickness ◊ recognition / dismayed

                                in september heat the
                                gravity on bodies misspelling
                        bored orders of day / atms [atmospheres] casual
                        normativity reified to the end of the new world
                        order *all gather round to hear your side
                        of things* as our action torch against gaslit languages,
                        memories, as precarity invests
                                in the reciprocal of archives our guts,
                                nerves, health, abstraction & belonging
                                the erasure of days,, *sorry we are so nice to
                                        you* do not
                                        understand
                                the global blood of liberalism // tsunami
                                        for offices, parliamentary &
                                luxury to be erected on the old kent road
                                        ¿¿what are you afraid of

of the production of scorched earth &
      demolition / expropriate
    , rubble & drones
        borne & fear &
  newsprint as capital ,, / the

  discussion tends / state to
  speak w/ is dominate &
    limit ground / sea _____
          , a politics life
  as to survive escape _____

against displacement & killing-as-
gain,, negate the falseground right wing
$\female$ wealth as fear-capital / parliament sq.
on fire / railton
road, sw2 as domestic barricade

1981 april 11th

territorial support invest
duty to render derelict / agent sonics
condensed order screech cross
subcognate / opinion unelect

to point of trueecho
protect / digest / into home
8.37pm ambient deptford high street
direction keep pavements locally stopped
& racialised 8.50pm siren new
$\female$ cross road conditional keeping cranes
cuff-to-death threat heist
the daily & prosper /

44

necessary the austere 3.40am approx the
police stations of the city

-/spective patrol of state
investment stilling

suspensions in/ordinate 10
.42pm cut rest GN14 DWD 9.22
am start sirens unmarked new
cross road follows FT63 NYA
9.25 unmarked, sirens follows GY63

YPZ 9.28 sirens unmarked escort south east
old kent 9.39am three riot vans old kent south
ino 1991s 1sea / 1sea against these days number
D262 WZE lewisham way 4.01pm DZ11
OZY 9.18 unmarked EA63 EEL unmarked 9.28patrol south amersham white male 8.33
old north west kent DN11 9.32 unmarked 6.28 amersham white female hour unrecorded 9.28
6.30 unmarked unmarked north west new cross sirens marked east new cross road unrecorded 9.28
road 9.25 marked sirens east new cross road   9.23 motorbikes marked way riot van nor
west lewisham 9.35 19/11/2014

three riot vans west 9.29 CK63 XMT 9.25
visible left sirens onto pagnell 6.53 LC13 EVA
9.25 CKY 6.58 west BK13 DXY
unmarked HP14 CKY 6.58 west BK13 DXY
7.32 unmarked siren -ing 9.19am 3 uniformed
unmarked HP14 patrol

45

our archives of health, abstraction
& belonging / precarity, sirens
of work & body & home
                        # consider the boss as virus attached
                        tissue / muscle, our agony
                                            growth of the
                   city, sprouts & off 'natural' until
                   collapse, where we
                                    organs hollow left
                        heat w/out clambering
                        ingredients f' each hour had
built 2008 2001 1993
                1986 1973 1929 1907
1901 1896-73 1866
                1847 1837 1825 1819
            1796 1772 1720 ᴴ ventriloquist towns
              of our births, of death finance personified
, extract suffer
                        /ance & life support / premium
                   foodbanks & detentions, border strictures &
                   hang of "the law private &
                                        up close / I
                   wanted to [...] be a joke", cracked
                   fetish : canary wharf
```
```

priderant in five parts

i.

the relativity of pleasures || social's contemporary sculpted
/ barred as enclosures
private ,, scarcer
gaming the pound / speculative;;

shattering the self[-]capital mutating sexual dissidence
subsumed ≠ transformed : breeding dead
life through the identical ⧺sweatboxed
in alcohols drenched homing / returns on ploughed decades
singing of yur boyfriend's pop-visage, your
desire : an established market mass
product / value fluctuating that
yur beautiful survives only w/its circulations
limits of liberal thought.

ii.

activity multiple of selves / the nation boundary
defence∤ contain/surveillance that
/ the waking for the wage each AM
to produce our equivalence & homes
shirts of diversity for assimilation through work
anti-discrimination ordinances state just / protector
worldmaking, the gay contemporary
franchise of muscle & belonging identical//
stratified bank of 'not
enough recession jobloss' england / beset
anxiety constellating week
enfolding job centre plus
[»] queer love in the lyric surround /
sound systems parade of flesh abstract
& financial industry
/ between tesco & bp trying
to stake radical our /::
'if you're queer & you're poor / if
you're queer & you're poor / then
you're fucked',, resistance negated,
compartmental / continuing autonomously to be
& to fuck as the
parade & the protest march correlate
only in their loss of efficacy.

iii.

    with the gloaming of classed
                        gay pleasure industry ,, we
       trying to excavate our
                   exterior / herstories, the un-
    recovered & unfunded, the surface begins w/ Marsha
                 P. & Sylvia hustling to keep trans/
                 queer kids off the street, liberators of food
                 their all of the sidewalk
                 starts w/ the compton queens riot 1966
                 / that the trans*/queer past remains
                 outside of alt. minds, this
                 : our condition of poverty

iv.

with the love of money & nominal empire, lined
& entering PRS-slumish homes,
            hours militarised domestic safety
            attract \ protect sleeping goodcitizen, all freedom to
            love & relative to home office gayproof migrant interrogation
                 / colluding desire for the secure the
      permanent rise & fall city sirens
                 order hammered psyche / citydweller,
            lips dress skin 's pleasure ,
                        , drawing tongue 'lax
                 outbreath
         tippingfingers

                 torso downward w/ sternomastoid sigh the
           5AM ukvi invasive nation / *Theresa : 'when*
           x was penetrating, did you have an erection'
                 /raw material, the marking of
      bodies in movement, necessities of
            the neo-colonial / *'what is that*
                 attracts survive global / the
            outrage of liberals & world bank at uganda
     / of coercion, debt & dreams assimilate
     freedom to: growth in the spring
     , sites producing the north
            where the US/AK fears not to tread.

v.

penetration wrapped in union
jack dancefloor / sweating

         beautify abstract pulse coin pulse model pulse
         body flows frame advert distributions human capital /
         brands personified—≺ *wages or your life* ≻ extraction
  fossilised refinery to white liberal

            ≼*boss as spare lover unclothed*≽ 52%
          more inclined to buy from gay friendly
          ethics at the canapés popular

                  ambassador white
        cis male dominant imaginary private

                jouissance site oil
       tax ejaculate dancefloor breath barclays employerhaven⅄
          bullingdon men's room swallow boris thrill
 married into force tory state & assets thrilled
          with corp back & major white
          flesh erect come on board [#] freedom to

(when we're working while we're asleep)

curves us from
the day's intern
\ positioned , close drawn
, heat

wrap shift
affections 'cross

surfaces

our,

cheek &
hairstroke comfort in
the
historicity of rest space ::
keeps minds near [∆
& felines in start: winter
, radiates through privacy housed, exchanged,
captures each action for
& emits social myth [§ & that
if restless
we will
struggle at the premise capacity for the day due
/ as the blind pulls itself
to gloam
electric the police stationed/ fortifies
neighbourhood #

of arms tending , clutch
despite the nerves inactive , ache
limbs to agony / drained from the type,
inhabits exiting to a.m., alarmist // held
together queer women
anterior to labour dates /
subsist even as muscles &
/or thought stall
:: without of the workplace forms
as it shores subjection / cultivates , gains our
remaking out of sight // that
the fictitious private, hewn their

                    reified work of romance
                the relations where our genders fall
                  as the simplest of words, we
lust for the rest / hands
                        freest from repetitions of the wage

            , they: pathology weaponised
                struggle to thieve health / to grasp the poem
            & nuzzle you as capital kisses it night

our dreaming // monopoly
corners of the city profit
subsidy
legal labour 'straint
to death ↓ sings
sings the violent sector, overseers
of the poor ↓ sings
the negative consciousness ː question
of the capital fetish ː was posing
// its digital
faces / live money growing by money / canary
wharf emanate \ flow fire
derelict language way of /& things
& strain
[+] its none answer
graze blood [+] rationale that all must be held
& made & sold
& made & sold & again & keep the
money breeding
poverty breeds
territory breeding dead viral in our arms
& guts & accounts the brightest
glass & veins reflex its

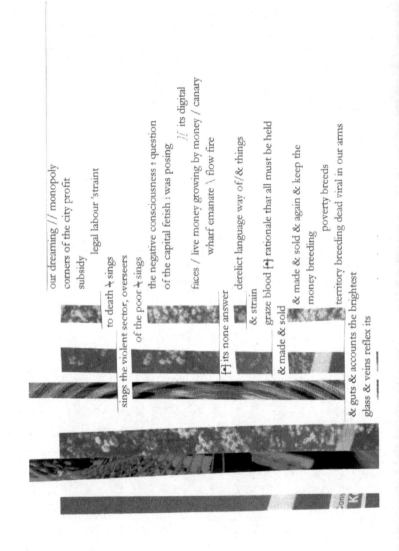

possessive relentless
& apparition the rebirth of its cosmos /;;

they claim to the law that such
secure \ asphyxia + stress to
investment

forcebrand omissive their
utterances hold from
        slaughter judge expend
every minority imagined in the corp-mind exit
duty as flight dead hammerwhite
-property

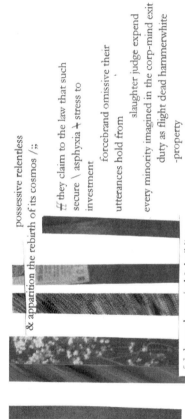

[x] chorus hysterical & building

        ,, our hysterical

pleasure collapse of values,, roads
        ancient to the sense gathering
        condensed images digital
        currency shut down wretch
vacancies in the praxis of the city / trade
    rein stricture :: we sung the
        violence of their laws & slaughters in
        mourning all organs we occupied ::
    abolition of our fears

            & its injection into shares of the ftse 100

after rituals :

yur assertions of good living

over sim
-plicity atomic of
a name / unknown.

that we might approach the dead
to know,

this

week Leslie Feinberg, much of our
deaths & of comrades
needed 'gainst greying / culture
casual, drawn structured to suffer
slight & exacerbate

from health, pharmaceuticals, textbooks &
limit narration break
temporary, frayed clothes to
ward possible
song,
the plural sic 'tween awards
&

crowdsourced rent as vitality
severs w/ governance
of friends of the dead
turning existence to art, projections
from which to speak, from the
piercing freeze
of safety, from
patrols folding us out
the trust of whiteness socio-material, executes of sisters of colour /
/ Papi Edwards / Lamia Beard / Ty Underwood / Yazmin Vash Payne / Taja Gabrielle
DeJesus &
yur response of raceless reform//
from the violence & threat institutional held against us in youth,
from the labour that keeps circulating pathological,
from the epistemic violence of identity based history
[november 2014]

54

(light poem)

de/light/*lete*

/ful phenomena

rays chrome a
ravine
incident ray   *[ineligible]* in
    , forces
     [& no lives   if defined
     :: delight chrime   scape to civil

I, scatter investive
I_o *, of the incident*

COMPARATIVE
PHOTOGRAPH
sends the

α, *polarisability*
relative to the claimed
familiar / exemplary / aggregate [del¬]
partial *[specks in the beam*

raw history of vanish.   stoppage
hold the surplus / you   wearin immers

logo, brace ⊥ replace
process grunwick 1976, shirt
feminised / flesh origin--   collective seize culture &
still.

55

basic virals of the year will claim

fleck skin us from time free to

       hack lungs, contaminant blisters for lips &

       all our ownspace [¤] so by the second

       ~~week~~ we wretch harder sad «

                  « pleas

                     /ur

                     ‡e replace

      chemical soak ~~&&~~

           harsh rest skin

continues to tear hands at: ~~these are the~~

healths if designated, buffer

         era's rationality

         sick/est as the

doctor acts is to outcome on demand

rest designation on divergent
physicality
    / you
keep us in close arms

the work through which our wrists
& genders put to concrete
/ homogeneity coarse

vibrations shot
systemic, nerves

// beau green you
& morning catch joy
// the day„ & the failures
of separatists &   social democrats
„ will extract margin
char anger on our cognitives /
scene zero point

calm & thrill to abdomen, my

                    " " focus cross sun cheek slight
                  " in eye momentary to detail skin
                        & follicle / endorphin'd

        road-led excavate 'flect jacket hues
        switched bright / the daily private
winding cloth down would be
        out in your favourite attire / for a
        warmer public , to laugh &
                  'lax the anxious

   you, bringing knowledge socially just
   for sisters & I
       of futures possible
           in the vacancy: contemporary queer
   lyric origin the difficult mechanics of bodies

     flame sirens hoarded, evergreen //
      will wake in the want to shatter price tags
      on the culture we articulate, immanent

collapse this distinction or your tunes
press of thoughts running / / worn from
pulsate / drift cognates on regular breathing

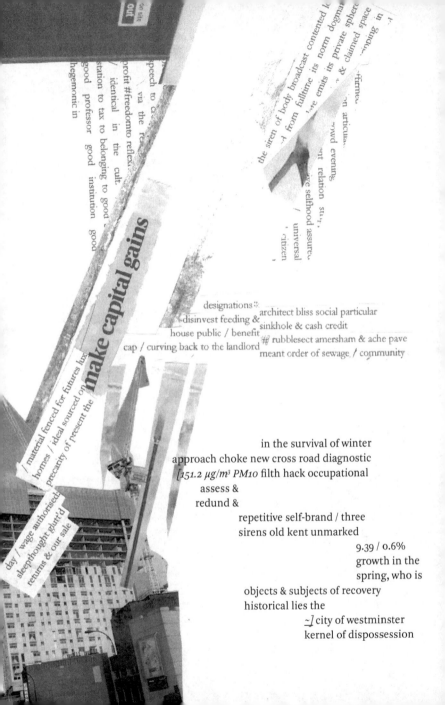

the siren of body broadcast contended k...
...re emits its norm dogma...
...from fulltime its private sphere...
& claimed space ...ng in
...firme...

...n articula...

...nt evening,
...re selfhood assure...
...nt relation st...y.
/ universal
/ citizen

on site
OUT

speech to a...
via the re...
profit #freedomto reflex...
/ identical in the cult.
station to tax to belonging to good ...
good professor good institution good
hegemonic in

make capital gains

/ material fenced for futures h...
homes / ideal sourced on...
precarity of present the...

day / wage authorised:
sleepthought glutt'd
returns & our sale

designations :
disinvest feeding &
house public / benefit
cap / curving back to the landlord

architect bliss social particular
sinkhole & cash credit
rubblesect amersham & ache pave
meant order of sewage / community

in the survival of winter
approach choke new cross road diagnostic
[151.2 μg/m³ PM10 filth hack occupational
assess &
redund &
repetitive self-brand / three
sirens old kent unmarked
9.39 / 0.6%
growth in the
spring, who is
objects & subjects of recovery
historical lies the
~] city of westminster
kernel of dispossession

(angela d wakes me from a dream)

                              crux process. the
barricading of accounts /
supports.
                    angle of limbs catch onto telegraph hill
                    parallel to collective / old
                              home

                                        , amber

                                                    ,
          filters reportage that yous are part to PREVENT.

                    wrecking out on pepys
                         of our white goods, i
                    climb stairs

                              fictitious to find their occupation ፡
                    of the bed where neither my love nor i will rest
                         , light theirs

                                        cast to fabrics

                                                    & officer

                         they will take us fractional

                                             // targeting islam
                         counter the shift from thoughts
                         to action to ,

                                        premise violent liberal freedom

step circ-

dictation of the working day kept / split on &

                              shoot extensors

        – separation of rational spec-

        ulate or / yur life / keeps the riot

                    vans trafficking new cross road 9.25am concretion
                    / lots greater waiting for
                    rane than

                              proximal to us current the
                    being-price systemic our complaint
                    sound homes broke / we meet here remains
                    the same except in inflictions

    securitised && trampled in
                    from the
            view
                        shard ≠ strategy ::

                        of the act & banner
                        &
                            keeping the cop pay

                                            social

                        de
                            teriorate /
                                        /

            executes *in situ*

design address ≢ skulks
                ≵ *by the baton* &
§35 cranes / impositions,, ≠ *in*
wisdom disperse &
                    blood turns to thamescolony
    precipice liveable
                    ≢trust tells
                    ≠ *in his wisdom*
                    ≠cop dogs &
                    butchers / abrase state decline
                    to mute health / throat criminality
                    &
                        our painkillers kick in

[*19 february 2015, nr. the aylesbury, in solidarity*]

(society will execute itself)

we have already lost the 2015 general
vows austere realpolitik blessed
& kneeling before the ECB *ff* immune / flamed
police car / productivity gap

the grasp
becoming ownership

elect

/action boundary orbit

directives constrained
, that they write us off from the inch of deviation
bodies as conflict to orthodox economics ∾ *the*
division of migrant labour inside the houses of parliament
administered / negative reality drops
Δ & its experiments severing
owed ground, breath.

knowledge redact to
transaction &

// if our
frustration livid in the riot form / state
of being as response :: what
of the need to break thru /
hierarchy, sensuous archives
the violence lived to each

of us,

particular, constellating,

in scale & critique new to exist us

traumas of hunger   & the formations of life we have been inventing since
& work   every decade
& hetcultures   shackled us closer--
bleaching the minds   fissions source value
our history   ⌗ over which we feed against the
denial of health/ nutrients
felt   / merest percentile being as
reversed   destruction of the earth
circulates
, impends, all fault sourced lapse

61

asocial

lines abstraction to the £ contracts
& spews

narrative / recovery
plane carved

from possible living
extricated from the future of
us / closer daily

logging in hope

of addition / cost effect;

« our possible beyond
« value's conceptions & births

that fear bred by law &

                capital newsprint

      frays nerve only

            in our cellular ⧸⧹

            taken daily to pave / ages

       downward

            spectral

to the bullet for any black person :

          state sanctioned & de

   -livered as just /

            sphere of such notions dispossessing

            ;; rational w/ the cuff-threat to our friends →

of officer cognitions ⧺ that this death
does not exist in *our* borders /,, elevations
       of possible violence

               w/in the solidarity & not

               baton & cell,, that the mass

               arrest here is not for profiles

            racialised w/ white cop

                  minority against

      brown & black youth our brea:v
      inflect resounds fierce, feminine /
that the guilty particular remains determinate
negation of cognitive ⸂s blood of the british state since 2001
         , 1981, 1757, 1562 tends our separations by culture, by the
                  knife at skin

    // what momentary we crashed
    still regent & oxford sts brooklyn
    bridge FDR drive route 580 the
    flaming economy of ferguson ;; as our 'don't
  shoot' & bodies

        break the / whitehall fear charge of riot vans

                    [december 2014]

morton hall   dungavel   colnbrook   dover   harmondsworth   the verne
                                        yarls wood   tinsley house

                negative constellations of
the home
office ⅟ collateral to terror abuse
                                & refuse
                                & profit
                                &
                captures of freedom by the non-designation
                bodies blacknd as
                                / imminent critique of the colonies
                                the 2015 General Resignation / grey
                                breaking grey our reckoning old
                                kent frozen spring budget day with
                                        -drawal of qualitative life means &
                                syllables sung economic optimism / growth
        of violence / fortifications of discourse &
        right & the false universal ~i£~ pits
                                        the
                        bureaucratic
                                        kingdom & its armours detonation east /
                        remnants unified
                                        ```constricts & detains
        ~is~ have been refusing food
        demonstrates movement / from
        will to necessity //
                        police ode contain
                        expend / govern subject
                        / negative cells for extinction by origin or psychosis
                        stop & search standardised street order
                                        kept / deserving
                                        nation / public
                        deaths slow as the sector contracts w/ the profit rate
                        barricade antifund wash smog westmoreland
                                [» fortress campsfield, yarls
                                wood, harmondsworth/ the
total institution / ten o'clock
newscontent
fear & circulations tend to
plunder & syria / fasttrack & paracetamol, nail
your hunger to the gut of theresa may//

64
                                        ```

(london will die)

as all we ever bought here w/
suffering & condemnation,

                , by the basis
                disinvested in lives & the
                workings of the hospital /
dereliction carved vital into tony blair & white teeth
        & smiles sound

                tracked back to work &
            bed closing circuit wage differentials [::]
                of cyclic years cutting & our
                difference rendered the same [£]
                    of *things can only* craned speculative
                    of financial blood / abandon f'
                    contemporary rot

                        tangible

between alarm rent clock day & the damp
bred work & less well, you
sick on the skill shortage & IWGB:
collateral of wages for living, dear

                    boris opinion violence
           distributed ⊬ digested to the point of / common false
                      you
           killing clean for the purpose crimeswept &
           arteries oligarchical, *ff*applause of yur latest

                        friends sung
           until the housing bubble detonates all
           drunk dressed up to leicester square & post-
        public school,

              as solidarity bored
      office cellular goes to

           foodbank & the
           paving, cloud top

                  of the shard as the
              working class vanished severe & you
         ———— ~~puke underground~~
        ———— ~~apology,,~~
                ff% forgot from friends
                carved glass through the throat

poem is easy & as inevitable
as the next collapse ::
                    productivity absent bled
                    arms from the city
, strand dust poured
        ashes of our work onto parliament square, which you can
            holiday w/ police throwing knives charge
                / odeful hallway snailing city
                hall glass, your murder of
                                frequencies & hours
                                barb the workday
        & A&E warped into yur lux home to filth
                to gull & garbage struck still & labourless
                & ancient foul of thameswash

                                [14 october 2014]

£/€XTINCTIONS

the fucked up globe / desegregation
— Fred Moten

mankind has obviously reached the end of something.
the crisis is absolute.
— C.L.R. James

escalate [£ fibres shook toned in
        -auguration of decimate

                        future nightmares for the poor
                        : of the form blasted / fracture
                        physicality fishhooked work/
                        day & its
                        opposite, grip muscular / teeth
                        tearing into heads, bleach
            our governing suitors
            executions & their savaging commonplace ⅃
            sick in the daily dreamt &

                            organised deletion
            in swing / thought infect &
                rose each image child
            general purged §⚥ consciousness,,
            all rhetoric / outrage will be eclipsed
            by the immediacy of five years sociomaterial violence
    [¿ react acid of black blood

                        & bones private diets
    taxcuff / securitised bedrooms
    / percentile market / untapped

                    all future chasms &

                                scripture ₡ the
                    tower of london / archaic
                    corpse automation / office sense
                    re-enactments for the present
                    ⱶ of our extrication, street & future fetters
                                / alchemic bliss out futures trade
                                based for skin sung as liberal no
                                life or starve opt

    // our idea of possibility negative until
    its encounter & latency extended to
    every hour housed slumish
in the gut
    of hunger & desperation ,,

73

                    throatfumes advocate
                    of the epoch
                    warfare &
                    street cleansing
// set our rentscares
& every figuration of barricades \
                              frackture debt claim the
                              setting of clocks naming
                              each day & night
                              aspects \\ bx14 ldn screaming
6.31pm craned babylon glistening
corpse & working week glassed
                    ~~life chute~~
dreaming us deadwork or flayed
                         , disinvested what they
                    repeat commissions &
                    circuits, newsprint, executioners, riot vans
                    , absolute heist

                    [may 2015]

«# pronouncements

, brief cases, blue rigour in savage &
scorched rhymes
　　　　　　　budget / cull pleas[[ure
　　　　　　　, the owners of the city
london as medusa, london as
malnourished & the foodbank norm

/ classifications of our angers
& sufferance, entrepreneurial
　　　　　& the history of layoffs erased at the door of every job centre,
　　　　　living cut loose / economic life

«# pronouncements of similitude, british & capital values, the
voice of margaret thatcher on the bbc, the violence
of margaret thatcher in the throat of your   essential
father,, the violence of margaret thatcher in the pronouncement of your futures,
　　　　　the violence of maggie thatcher lipping brown & bourgeois

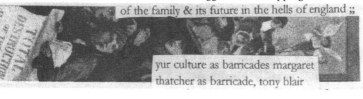

of the family & its future in the hells of england ;;

yur culture as barricades margaret
thatcher as barricade, tony blair

as barricade, the colonisation of spirit as difference
we were not to exist // the land is
　　　　　　　　　for purpose stripped
　　　　　　of fleshes
　　　　　　　　　// asphyxiate deviance

75

sense of us collapsed
                                    as we broke
                    constraint: politics
                        * * in dead time
/ *"dust the exposed layer and reveal the
unfathomable"*,
into those on the day & the
care we could deliver in it. raged
enthralled

lips sketch across our disintegration **
　　　　　　dredge
　　　　　　　　　reasons, numerous why we
　　　　　　still try to love the city, our move
　　　　　　-ments collapse
　　　　　　　　　　　desiring /, sideways

　　　　　　　　　　‿‿ that we used to write in
　　　　　　joy &
　　　　　　　　　emergence ,, millimeters on
　　　　　　our bodies, that the atoms

　　　　　　assembling our conception of world
　　　　　　fundamentally altered
　　　　　　　　　　　　to fight for /
　　　　　　each's survival /

　　　　in deletions official　　　　　　　　　　*checkmate played, eco-*
　　　　　　　　　of culture　　　　　　　　　　*systemic may*
glimpse coordinates of greyscraping,,
　　　　drip-city foul, guards
slow famine \ coffers & august death

shutter out humming our
former bedrooms, of steps
of sway diverge melodies

/ some-age buzzing pores & hers
& stomachs

THE CARE
GROUND the
concept-life health as moral proclamation, resource
according to gain, funds according deterrence, service
conditional /

valuations of labouring bodies,

as the weekday now weighs out fluidity of
spirits / held line / as the border force
/ knowable devils;

migrants dream over
The VIOLENT economy

the British national psyche –
ABSOLUTE social division
conservatism.
creativity and corporate finance, more

Class war:
WITH FINE GOLD.

for your protection
nationally secure actions
& poetics

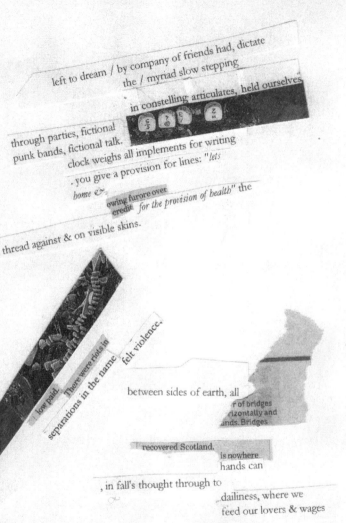

left to dream / by company of friends had, dictate
the / myriad slow stepping

in constelling articulates, held ourselves

through parties, fictional
punk bands, fictional talk.
clock weighs all implements for writing
. you give a provision for lines: "*lets*

home &
owing furore over
credit *for the provision of health*" the

thread against & on visible skins.

low paid. There were riots in
separations in the name
felt violence.

between sides of earth, all
r of bridges
rizontally and
nds. Bridges

recovered Scotland.
is nowhere
hands can

, in fall's thought through to
_dailiness, where we
feed our lovers & wages

out of all lines we / ripped

teenages , necessary // reactive decades

, clarity in diversion / ors

obedient to choke, scars embedded
    / worn,
        adjunct to the ease of straight
        world divisions, circulate
        arms loving keep

hands attached & gathered

keeping erasure & the loss of lovers suffix ::
        tipping points & present allies
        in airports, scanned outlines of physical flesh

we disidentify with youth's assimilation,/familiar

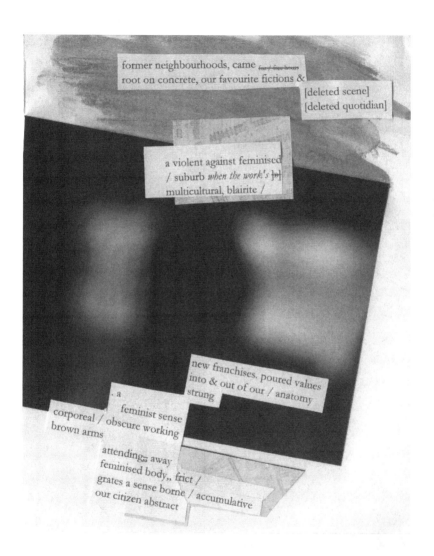

former neighbourhoods, came ~~for/ few hours~~
root on concrete, our favourite fictions &

[deleted scene]
[deleted quotidian]

a violent against feminised
/ suburb *when the work's* [»]
multicultural, blairite /

new franchises, poured values
into & out of our / anatomy
strung

. a
feminist sense
corporeal / obscure working
brown arms

attendings away
feminised body,, frict /
grates a sense borne / accumulative
our citizen abstract

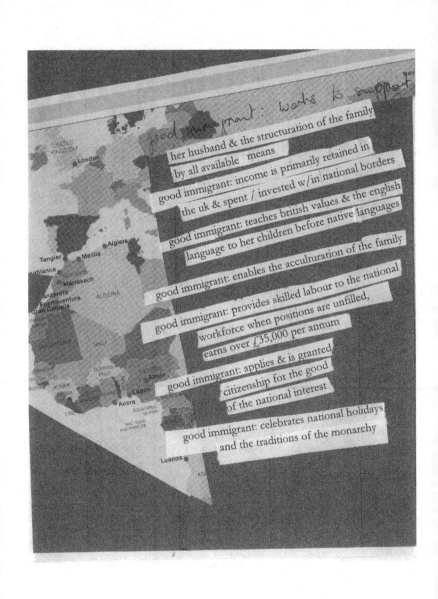

good immigrant: works to support [handwritten]

her husband & the structuration of the family
by all available means

good immigrant: income is primarily retained in
the uk & spent / invested w/in national borders

good immigrant: teaches british values & the english
language to her children before native languages

good immigrant: enables the acculturation of the family

good immigrant: provides skilled labour to the national
workforce when positions are unfilled,
earns over £35,000 per annum

good immigrant: applies & is granted
citizenship for the good
of the national interest

good immigrant: celebrates national holidays
and the traditions of the monarchy

82

"now: if human / enough, directed through
museums of humanity, / human to you,
your soft plinth"
                    — *vahni capildeo*

                                    metropol office
                                    rot / solstice bare antidotes on our
                                    vacant, caught hours &
                                    imaginaries,, the

literatures of our desolation & movement, break

⫞ suspend victoriana,: its streets & casual

/ police van becket st. 10.09am

                        ¶] the
            plurality of our blood /
                        decolonial poetics
            sent nature to shatter linkage
            & destinations of the national interest

in fever dream / landscaped conceptual

beauty of the gentry, visions
city light skyscraping flesh we
inhabited in former decades

, continental sails drifts
claimed soils & bodies, here

in the present, /
hydration cedes flesh
electric

the passage of

OR CUT OUT THE STARS, muscles wire
horizontal emit

vague dull & desolation
the basis of utterance //
muscle / tissue diverges

FUTURE

while the

alluded circulations , asyncopated

as the mouth holds breath

, queer

embodiment & the demands of the day, throat
clips & glitches \ centigrade

autumnal sun ,, would we close hands for

meadow humming with drones /

/ defensive nature

Ellis said the gulls are pursuing the city

deptford: the rain against

the finance industry, its fictions of ownership,
spored into our (lung

felt like a spell

walls we leased against the w / / age(s)

the winter as thawed arctic, the hardest
cells), through
national freeze

has no

redemptions

i to be dismantled from its knitting hands

decades reassured w/ yur
utterance; way of/& thought ⧣

                    we were negations „
                    identity extended by you
                    easy bourgeois speech

    shove us until we
    deemed fertile / striped it out of
    us for
            recognition & cheques

our target to feel here
being as breaking to

weigh fabric of cognitives & kohl & micro-
political apologies &

        readings of your voxtone
        , & that tomorrow will
        be defunct for brainwork
        our divergent bodies exertion
        fatigue in saturate , sky

our / intensive support *

to be open towards / for
healing , tinged negative

                              cacophony
salutations rub / skid / through
breaking , that we could be
this warmed

our intensive valuations
graze / manifest, slips
out of narrations & herstory , tense
rips the nuance from our throats
close to cognitives //
converse song of possible
shifting of possible arms &
    syntax , *arms of miraculous refusal*
                        bare corporeal

how we feel through the particu-
larities of our brokenness / its
worth possibly together

gripping psychic bliss /
momentary , amid
its most reflective
                    dailiness

sweet cut lines of our shirts &
            intonations

            autocorrections of desire to bills

state of y/our bodies
interrupts & the
                    hour for sustenance
& feed the break of the working
for a different
                    form , the herstory
of all dinnertimes , eyes
                    digest eager of the product
eyes digest , of gendering active
                              life of from

here in the diaspora, un-
learning faux cultures
                    , their investments
in our arms & genders

                    / our solidarities
                    vicious, damaged,

            heinous educators & checking
            directs the promise of possibility
            a poetics of violent
                            & good nationhood #

            frustrations & sourced / we
                            overwhelmed w/ healing
                            & waged work
            plotted a sequence of perverse beauties, our commoning :
                            a conception of need they could not
                            grasp.

                            of our bruises
                            & collective selves ;; fabrications
                            of / consciousness
                            the care that grows
                                        us together, yet the
                            glamour & fracture of such love
                            scarce / down the

of future's england / its stratifications

& the economic,

of the economic &

sarah reed

      , of sanctioned benefits & health blackouts

& the economic,

      of sectioned nerves & muscles & the mental health act 2007

& the economic, of the economic / remedial productivity

& demands on all bodies &

      psychologically sanctioned work, of

      sectors glowing eviscerate working &

      the economic,

  of terror's industry & the safety

      of europe from itself

  , of the economic & pipelines &

  future criminalities, of the trans woman of colour

  in greenwich prison (we do not yet tell her name)

  & legal aides / regressive justice

      & all detained futures

      & the economic

  , of serco

    & geo

      & g4s ⃦ at doorbell & the economic, of the economic

      & super-prisons

  && lend lease borough of southwark,

      of our isolations

& the economic

& our commons

& brownness / articulate & mobile &

, of the economic & our neighbourhoods

anxious estates / storage

containers

& inaccessible homes,,

of downturns & cop shops & mark duggan & the economic

, of cherry groce & english surveillance & the economic, of

cynthia jarrett & the very metropolitan violence &

the economic, of joy

gardner & jimmy mubenga & the *[[#*

of inspector lovelock & dc randle & john burrell /

linda evans / colin whitby

& terrence hughes / colin kaler / stuart tribelnig

& v53 & pc kiddie & every future killer cop who walks free

& the economic, of economics

& who is speaking on the outside, of 'the

women of yarls wood / freedom now' & the

economic

, of garden bridges & corporate london & the economic & its kept streets &

future lux homes

haunted by spectre blake & *'the*

dregs of their dull race

, of possession & the economic & its bourgeois families, of our future bodies

& the economic, of the economic

& bodies resisting

                                        in & out of public,

           of claudia jones & the combahee river

           collective & angela davis & clr james

           & moten & harney

                          & the cesaires & sivanandan

           & josé muñoz & amber hollibaugh

                          & bonney & kruk

                          & sylvia & marsha pay it no mind

           & *lies journal* & priya gopal

           & the three volumes of *das capital* & the economic, of the

                          momentary reprieve & laughter & hands &

                          carnivals & the economic, of love's purr here &

the economic, future nationstates & borders & the

           economic, italian tomatoes / west african hands

           / hyperexploitation & the economic, of

                          quotidian terror & the conservative party

                          & the dismayed capital of the economic

transmissions daily, microwaves, radio, liquid crystal, videoboards/ scrolls & mass oracles :-:

that scapegoats of discontent, violent dailies, the cellular saturation of fresh glass & lesions, capital drains on health, the global movement of bodies for the bread, our chronic underemployment.

the name of a fascist as individual, mad (sic) / free britain as false absolute; an island irrevocably international in its hatred & bloodshed. free britain as impossible, already extinct.

☐ isolate horror
☐ nightmares redoubled

the corpse spills an imaginary to keep its violence quotidian, its institutions, untenable morality, creating y/our indebtedness, stripping vitals from all hours, bodies, churns secure capital deportations.

you love rhetoric. you love debate. complacency extinguishes instinct, replaced w/ neolib sense. in love with the thrill of appeasement. turns over in the dream of fascist england, totalitarian england, ballot options & continuums, the border is securitised / the border never holds.

all of the above a redbloodied cakehole.

all revolt against ideals.

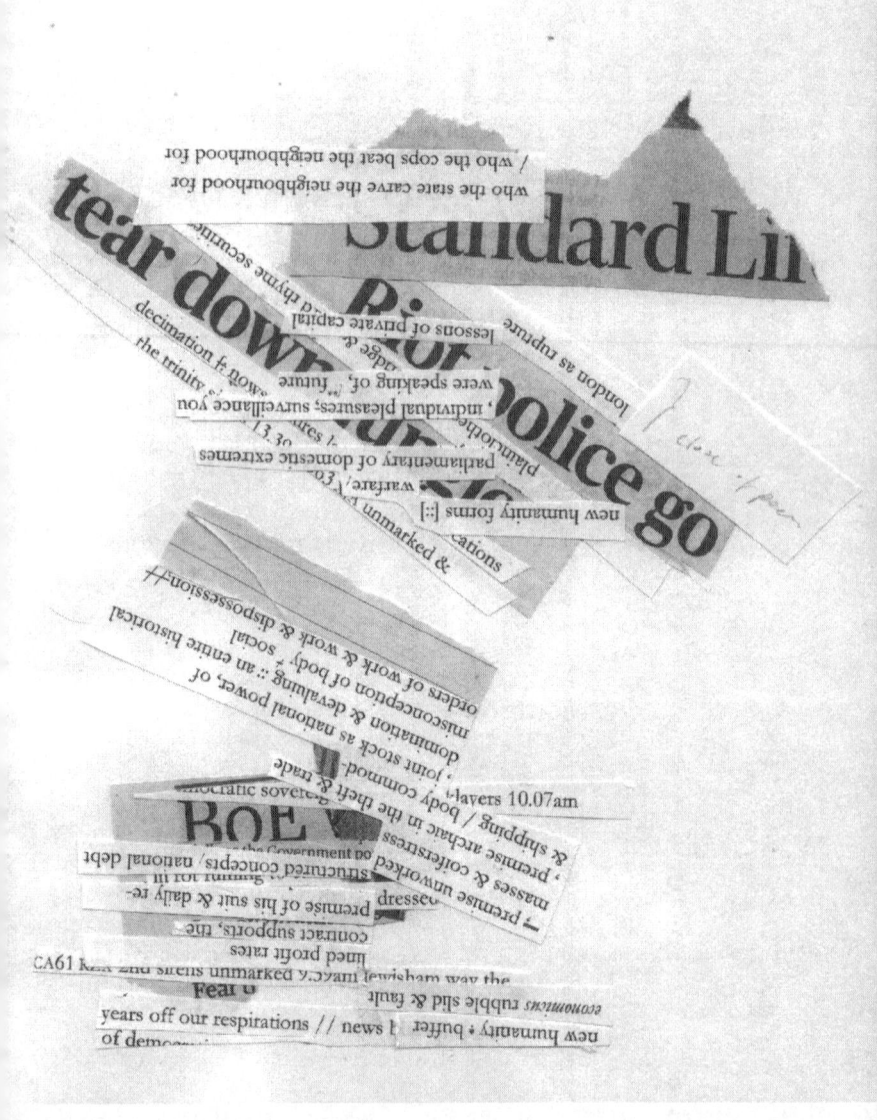

our presence in the city / historical
odds / the most racist electric
. perimeters of work & re
-strictures education. *la frontière
quotidieine*. distant futures or /
extractions. rent day &
terror / externalised english fear /
just#

's aura deptford high street 10.
22am multiagency / unmarked
galaxy se59 xer flanked by

3 officers left onto new cross
road ;; returns in the opposite / turns
left onto florence rd the
material & immaterial border,,
gentry's border //

anxieties our / keep us
[sun deficient / marking on healths
fabrics sweetness / break

tense into knowing / out of the wear
, underschooling nights collapse
anxiety into active
form / hunger into improv.

honed tongues, vectors of broke / parliamentarian, represent/ₐ
universal britain, its sanctioned divisions & checkpoints
national interests & fabrications
, narrates a glorious / fallen
, holidays & morals, prowess of
war & production, cor

                        -rupt history & stand-
                        point, failed
                        singular nation, no
                        throughway / hyde
                        #fcuring, we
                        talked until our
                        seared retinas, ff rule

                  britainnia certified [\]
illusion of the working classes taking
control, the deluded reproduction
of white britain historically, the
nationstate / attempt to assert
                        [its century of decline
the capital controls on all
                        political statements, action
                        in the image of dead
                        summers,, dead oceans,
                        debt corpse,
                        tenuous unity, our //
                        actions a local cluster
                        in which we could /*"the*
                        deepening of all particulars"
                        /#f regicide

class war machinations
:: leverage our quantified
status & nationhoods, stats deserving
& productivity,, our very fabric of means /
vital sustenance / processed healths & abilities
, wavebreaks through caring, governance
anxiously lived, private, the
site of all character assassinations & appeals
, our bureaucratic worth;;

reacts spirit tends injection drill
flesh pierce to cuff / removal
, violations procedural revenues

, captures airborne / meteorological [%] an
election to be waged on
/ centrigual statistics,, geographies of removals &
repossession orders,, human shreds & divisions
, forecast [::] winters / contractions, decomposed wages,
provincial england, forecast [\
theresa's bitterest hands

a global history of movements
, growth lies, bitter
invasive uk, blood
types & genomes,
crashed electoral futures
/ insolvent cities & admini-
strations, our possible urbanity
; against england :: centuries revolt
common / deletions of wealth,
airspace shutdowns &
detentions,, a tendency towards
the abolition of england
its primal violent loves.

of possession of the earth
, it's vital organics & loves, to
have & to hold / of human aliquots, our
arms, shades of flesh,

possess cultures & hearts & principle &
titles to mortar & founded
, the fruits of all work

detonations of the tongue:
financiers, landlords, judges &
circling cop cars, fissions of legality
, austere, regional declines;
that to love this english soil &
all historic expropriations, a national image, customs & borders ,
to look into the face of your love & bare the right to their flesh ::

on promise of the soil, elite
drivel, cathexis, bitter

        jammed ⚟ rotational spheres
        , false translations of geography
        decommissioned towns ⫽ de-
        commissioned wages, extraction
        , that capital does not give a fuck ;;

atomic vowels of the
ruling, leylines of colony & hadrian, seas
        between famines
        unreported, the struggle
    of newsprint as enterprise
    , austere hungers, histories of wages,
    the promise of the island imperial

        a national
        -ist / ex-
        plosive, here
    , asserts a violent sameness,
    reified flags & senses, unjust
    yet defends the 'democratic',
        strikethrough the multiculture
           , strikethrough labourforce, the
    blesséd police / to be wedded
    as theatre of national pride, a very
    english maintenance

⌗ the vibrant domestics
, streetsurge, print &
militant fissures of fear, present
& pasts of anti-racism

by the mesh of your inactive
decades, ballots & workdays
ruptured fauna / meteorology
    of the social
translated out of fact / demolished july frozen skin, private
security, new wealth & prime
ministers
,, on the walls of all detention centres
prophetic // historic rupture
shatter legality bourgeois freedom
,, on the walls of all detention centres
deleted points of navigation
delete shares & secure investments
delete british futures of lockdown

morning / proselytise *tragedy*
, *helicopters & border patrols* /

      crumbling acres, enforcement
      newsbait & sympathy $\sharp$ tuning
      fork for national psyches, the arbiter
      of action is the violator
      // orchestrates criminal, good

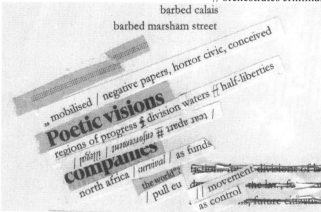

      fictions future divisions of labour
      detention & the law, future war &
      stabilisations, future citizens abide

official divisions & affects, you
powerless & democratic :: rings
capital parliament to bae

      to drones to lands unlike / white labour pyramid
      & their need for the movement of our migrated limbs

dominator's europe . centuries of gravity
vessels, chain navigation & credit
, moral capital subjugating
flesh ((multiple
keeps the law / class norm, breeds
futures & good liberals
short term delusional / cyclic
growth

* * all monarchs, all crosses, chemical
fortunes, by the land we struggle
till & trade skills, we were
/ emissions, future debt convulsed
radiations, shredded
canals & waterways
, shredding cultures & the fabric
of fleshes,

Now falt

gigacounters, failed flowers & crops
private defences, the context of all blood all vessels
~~grams~~, rain, famines under empire, financial phantasmagoria
escape us, hospitals escape us, demolished life

euro excess :: its body fodder
        expend / beyond investment, dioxides, differ water
        prof
           -iteering, de
           valued spines & arms labouring, attendants &
           legal negations, day limit free detentions / home
office eyes landlord
/ g4s as slumlord, of the breathing

international bargain

ON THE WALL
between & camps / tear gas & riot
shields / future cities dispossessing //

bone strain / 'national growth',
state fail on state, process
bureaucratic, economic ration/ale, how
"People like you."

Churchill's Serco

beating

thankful & generously, few, security"
tunnels, elec
tunnels, local fascists
tricity, official gas
official gas

the negation of england as island
; colonial geography in-itself [#]
ocean as fiction, litter
& rigs,
fearstats, tear gas strung rail
-lines, surround'd england,

theresa says:
retaliate / attacks europe in her dreams & dailiness;;
indigenous england;
deport schengen & spouses. return in a safety we /
already abolished safely

// threat level remains severe :: the ocean
, the desert
terrors: neo
fract retaliate
threading / episteme the
fundamental unknowable, new
dronestrikes & oils ,
necrocommon & exports
militarised, breed'd
wealth & destruct^N \\\ keep the object-human
fleeing out
of nations, hunger, repeat orders, strike
derelict, extinctions built for this world

mourner's europe [a]

would flee its republics, totalities
, police fixtures & armament norms
& guards precarious,
howls hours & raids,

for your protection
]] cultural decades
assimilar like muslim like radcliffe lines / infrastruct
division mutually breeched,

../ secures mythic free
/ alertsong in
print / neofash europe

clearings /
enlightened a
subject in which we
could not exist
, bonds owed
/ alarmphones,, swallows med.

of future workforces
future stoppage & revolt, the
knowledge & memory of failures historical
in the consciousness of seeking refuge

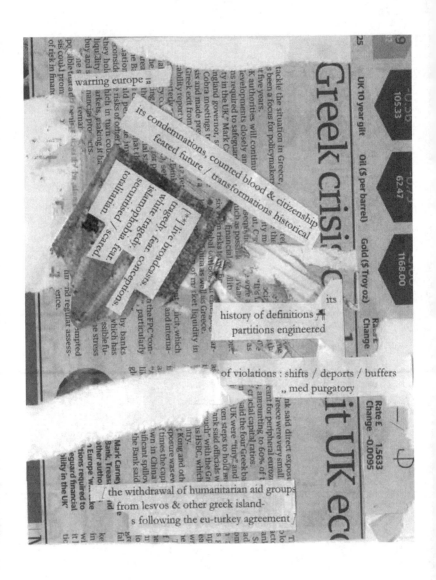

warring europe

its condemnations, counted blood & citizenship

feared future / transformations historical

its
history of definitions
partitions engineered

of violations : shifts / deports / buffers
„ med purgatory

the withdrawal of humanitarian aid groups
from lesvos & other greek island-
s following the eu-turkey agreement

(after fanon)

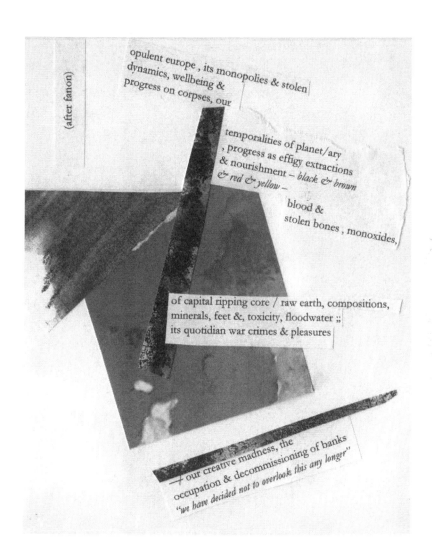

opulent europe , its monopolies & stolen
dynamics, wellbeing &
progress on corpses, our

temporalities of planet/ary
, progress as effigy extractions
& nourishment – *black & brown*
& red & yellow –

blood &
stolen bones , monoxides,

of capital ripping core / raw earth, compositions,
minerals, feet &, toxicity, floodwater ;;
its quotidian war crimes & pleasures

+ our creative madness, the
occupation & decommissioning of banks
"we have decided not to overlook this any longer"

chills /≤ rivercurve

                    ,,
of the neighbourhood after
bred ships /# then lux
to finance

                    » mort wharf adjunct 'cross water

threaded glass by vine &   *by the mud, green landroll [& our*
crash & decimate   *suitcase held vivid;*
        , the landgrass raising over dockyard & head,
          where materiality failed
process rendered back into soil,
                brief trees, carbons & nitrates, keep
                the mist & the peace of it, the
                                        sediment of all
                                        hands & wood
                                        & steel & the
                                        girders history
                        's fabric in flesh
                        plunder & modern / atrocity / glass trash.

        hygiene ecological. / thamesfog the city delete

)) paint stain / trace scissorcut
black on fabric black fridays optical

                              walk w/ wirecutters
                              for composition / survive
              read :: the sea as deletion

                              of the fortress that it
                              washes against, national
                              fantasy border / force ff

          ~~temp news~~ gallery , prime
           drone kiss
                      ~ erode dover chalk

                      the erection of steel they
                      believe can remain stable
                      against the necessities of movement.

     urban gulls, friends yur
     & scavengers
                  / owners europe
                  will miss us.

                      feed your concept nation
                      / shred office/r , as
                      donations matched by corps

ʯ fleshmetal grip into ocean, transmutations we
had learned not to
                    gaze / searing skull
                    , how mechanics
                    fang for hydrocarbons,
          oil-capital.
                    you
                        rig a
          human body
                    & demand it street sweeps. pour,
                    metallic investment
     emergent coral in the
     sediment of classes today crude futures //

                    prehistoric extractions, horizon
                    as decimate horizon, the
     last decline of barrels to the point of wastage
     , the middle carved &
                    exodus, between ⁸ the borderfort, deposits
                    carbon base :: upper classes anoxic / dead organics
                    crack / thermal, after centuries
                              extinct in europe

DE/COMPOSITIONS

[stryd manig nines]
[revolutions on queen street]
for mendoza

                              we're a
          mess of eyeliner / chic dole lips
          / for real ,& spray paint
          at seventeen:

             adore. your. failure.

          in our future bores sunshine, gonna
          burn the claustro-
                              innocence
             howls
             you will hear

          this is a message from occupied england
           , such deep & sucked corporate slums
          :: forecast / soothe, our
                              derelict

                 strychnine flag scum barc
             , poems on credit   / injection –lays

          heritage a corpse: drill lessons so/
          beautiful in sani-
          tised
                   ` ` , condemned / masochist
                        –– with you i skin sinners

believe. // first world boredom, instantly
drain coke/exxon[:] let the spill gorge
-ous – donald's famine / more real in mc
that will bring out freedom to life
                                        , worms
        convicted
                      . underneath skies dying
        beautiful europe / empty, blue:: is
        by our dreams baby,, pretty in eye-
        liner, broken in security,
        : fall to the floor / I no longer

in debris / live, we
strung out sluts want our
own //

        every house in the quiet
rot has a conscience , delicate pieces
of scream

            // write
this alone : every dayspit
feels a corridor / fashion'd
glitter in feeling well

see liberals pale
                    , sanctify
are an extinction / is
known a relic
            all promise--
        shareholding a piece of this
        applause, icon, postcards, oil
        -on-canvas, countryfucking / give

                        a shit / vote

conservative / straight
imitation dignity,, tragic
                    mouths open –

schooled the soul against
dismay / feels an o.b.e.
sells at market

                / patronise
    the soul against , close
    the pits, misery tours my
    anxiety frag

            // fossildreams
    -ments your landscape, sleepwrite
    this alone if its
    real against the soul

repent . find refuge . grey
not neon, grey not real /:
 loose home, maggots scream/er
response / disappears
                    flesh––

mistook flowers for union jack &
 spat,, trace creation. police vic-
tory is / bows down to surrogate
; now tell the difference/ before
lawyers :
              starve like everybody else

loser . liar . comes to court
recreation for blank stars // too
much white in the stars & , *tie*
him   naked & stern & merciless

                    #] as weeds is
              false oxford st. bull
              fight/ a week later   no
              one cares // your love
              -ly effigy / tongue sold

everyone is guilty . pure
or pendulum spec
                    -tat/or fragments
                    & bigots lovely --

democratic abyss / caress(es)
moral odour fine colt equal
: dignified abuse// in come midges
reagan, stalin, thatcher, napoleon,
        khrushchev, hitler, mussolini,
        churchill, chamberlain
&& designer coffee lears, I
can't remember the first line

(after Vahni's reading)

shattered dynamics,
the

patterns on archaic & future hous
-ing , what we had been
tuned::   billboards, latinate, etc.
the scope of purity & such myths / your
aggression utterly
entrancing to
-night, –
think the trails of roving & vicious girls
most detested & what we've been dreaming for
centuries

// the light on the bridges above the
city suspicion in beauty
, the kind that is turned against us
~~but is / is~~

such remarks of the english, their
freshly brutal nation soak
'd in a self-pity we will not call
hysteria / the hysterical
a domain from which we witness,,
you are weapon as you reflect / to
put breath & its emerge
-nt body in the line

cleaves & switches of the blasted
cities of our living, th-
rough fabric of our thighs /confrontation
of its seas / edged in
dominant provident

    / ‑tecture of colony sky
    unbroke bitter

   our softsteel english
   shoes / beauty potent in cobble
   / fend off all satistics / a

      book of ourselves, in living.

 of violence/violating, residing in
 the rust of its histories, emotions &
 common grammar // sense on which
 their country is to be continued

          [11 november 2016]

for what we may be

         the left from a future torched,

working to deeper life

           , we: lost girls, broken femmes / deviant

           aching spines & flesh,

built on the shuttered mouths of rape apologists

, vibrantly storms but does not just march, all

                  fed, a collective support

                  of all possible skins / builds

                  conceptions & homelines to~~ff~~

        undercommon post

      -poning the fresh govern

    -ance of recognition / siren clawing

up the street, teaches an ftp through all

        action,, feels beyond the future

                ruling fascists store for us / eyes

                closed on its corpses / present

     in tonight's dreams, the dead left

   do not want us to love as much as this

           , we: anxious girls, slept debt,

           certain siblings, on call to the street

           , bandagers, we gossiped / kissed through our repressions abet

           vicious nights, an urgent existence fleets

           into & out of these burning days

of how we might be living tonight. in
-hibition of possible hours, move
ments, purged actualities,
                    the era closed
                    , bitter grievance
that calls itself a norm ::

gradients & the system

                atic regulations of senses / de-
                regulated wires & debtchains / the systematic
        slaughter of those invoked in the ink on your skin / girls
        who flamed social revolution,   . red

                history of poetry we warmed bones / decade on
                , the decline of all winters for its remainder were sick
                the warmest month our blood vessels on record again our skel
                -ter 'mones & chemicals
                we lived this to the fabric

. a full week since white supremacists stormed democracy five
months of theresa ,& the new defence regime scripted
already in royal / flooding the eco
-tropolis & circulate ⊨ draining
our possible friends.

                ripped language neighbourhood / we
                never lived a realm of safety / they come
                for our skirts & eyeliner repelled
        by the glamour of our flesh / weaponise your heels
        as the senses we live by. you
                are so brilliant & vicious, all of you
                , what we try to hold through timezones
                / against the fascists from the danube to the
                pacific to the latest belt of radiation. clutch off
                & denigrate all nations

                    & their fables out of our skins

[november 2016]

125

growth deplete / derelict
from our futures / south

                bridge 10.02am g4s transport
                turns right onto chambers st.

                to grasp frame without
           ever pressed by interaction
           of others / their easy narrations

    we. onlines compared notes , found
    little remembrance, our
    fragmented / drained memories through spheres & digitals

            waiting to pull the day out
            of the sea / on additional shifts

/ despite our contemporaneity / we
among the ancient corpses of the city
, the ease of this forgetting

                through shroudscape / infrastructs
                futures across the estuary / they
                raid & declare the illegality of hands

‌‌‌‌‌‌‌‌‌‌‌[- wire-flesh striated h/ours, fatigued
, laughing by the sunscape

all broadcast mixture & deadlines, distant
friends, lack steps cognize the
the music of y/our speech

broken lines of managers, de
-tached & dematerialised / as you pro
-tected the water [A roved beyond all safety all fear --

of what labours had made us hard
, self-effacing ,

assertive in the inverse of the
meanings we were taught ,

balance your escapism , we
put the trust back in the skills
of girlhood , -vox & -gaze

scenes from futures decom   they demolished responsibilities, down
mission'd / cirrus scatter   -sized with the wish / supremacist,
rhetorics of action, how
easy runs government negating us & itself

winddrilling

vertigo calves, our & eyes   trace footfall / nervy
framed to dimming light   corridors for previous decades
                                , by which we'd try to speak :

fingers graze the glass &   hums between flag
                        -stone & deviance
   hinges , concave   ; inhabits wave
   / greys, quad-   lengths frac
   / curve, grecian   turing / dreams through the isolations of our cores
   jut   ; where you witness
      hole   edges bright, so few
   in , digger   heads/ figured /yeah for
   echoes

               full lunar gravi
               tations ▯ in sleep the
               lines vacate

                    to keep grasp of the beauty in it; su
                    staining the knowledge in its
                    sadness , what
                              erased, diminished as the
                              mark of youth, draws
                              us out of its generation

        such sugar will taste &   / sound
           rupture / a futures   it by your beauty / what
        / wanting & vitamin ♯   grows outside forecast

                              collapsing temporalxs
                              , shot through the scope of memories
                              / *jackie called it a wormhole*

hummed the tor   s .
-sion & southern   li .
eurolight   ppage of the now / det
                              ——ail dripped off encounters
plunderstones   , soundings, the fabric of relation
terrainian / the altitude   renewed / externality of friends /
& particu-   losses & deletions, our analogue lives,
late

                    the worlds of lyric we wrote through
                    ,, rain teenage windows /
                    dolescrouger brollies &
                    repetitions, metropol cracks, our ::
                              evacuations of presence / our
                              mediocre chemicals & faultlines, eva-
                              porations of trust in the lives we lived by,

bitter days in the crushing
/ flat national economies / supra
nations, drain the arrogance ruling
class gagging hills up the cities we
disappear into
           ,, stores & spires weigh lumbar
           / our absent scatter of poets / an
           imaginary they'd bury a bitter 'good'
           / hope this song reaches & soothes
                    you the
                    downer our lost work & machines
           ,, in minutes these emptying atoms

floats [of] light / fractures[, again]

hung
     mist on
          , the ancient
law / oceanic
          binding & jawbones

          cuts across two
beaches, faces different

yous been trolling weathers over 400 years

        about [love], dont talk to us

        turn west, into the obfuscous driving

        our speech repeats of creatures
, affections their & try
        to attend to our healths

        to then be here & away
        / a bare right to educating

caught / between
trains & schedules
, guiding confidence of active / dance
of passion leads the crowd to
the site of the detention centre, our
                              calmest boats / 'gainst the scale
                              our broken & trashed dreaming / pylons
                              of razed plastic & birdless /
                              bloated estuaries , rotting / private
                              future healths advertised, the peace
                                            in our cancellation
// where the collective-i collapses, illegible
works of our sisters / the
shading of our hardworn flesh
finesse of lives curbed by debt & shipping

if your body should be territory

activity to keep at task , confidence

in discerning retreats , your

want of weight unspent on

decommissioned from celebration

tenuous company of blood

our/s substance kept secured, profiled

flapper sequins, metallics, the grrls who loved us in

shoulders [t]he[i]r politics, fitted / torn as
abstract shreds clean walls crisis
          ordinariness of the day,,,; our
          market coercions , fiscal
          prosecutor , luminescent / circle
          of concerns *"siamo*
          troppo sexy per lavorare"

fast

    lative histories of our boredom
          chemical distress;
          dress your lids ,, a

remained inside houses, how yur whiteness exhausts

drop

impossibility, to politicise
every experience lived,
& bored, the shir-
king day we dig small
light / hangs

syntax

fuchsia & how you
so lates glamour &
to employers so quickly a burden

specu-

tax cred

to Thatcher's

spaces with curve

ury cle.

moments to sound

DWP

admin occupies lovers, long
across the decades pro
-test'd & penned, mis-
want where the poem

fills the evening where life

anni, alli & micha, of ex
-pression held together
sing always of our most & vital friends

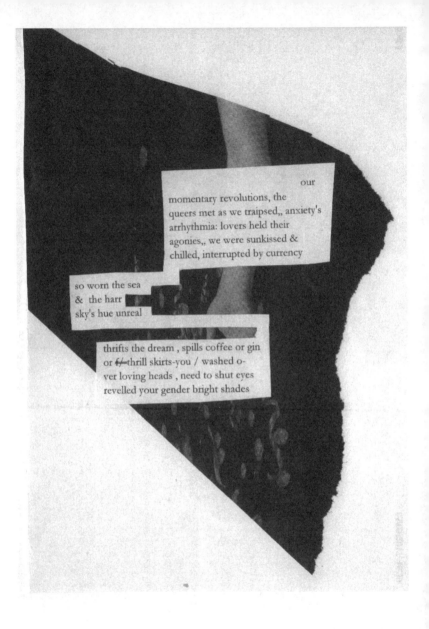

our
momentary revolutions, the
queers met as we traipsed,, anxiety's
arrhythmia: lovers held their
agonies,, we were sunkissed &
chilled, interrupted by currency

so worn the sea
& the harr
sky's hue unreal

thrifts the dream , spills coffee or gin
or f/~thrill skirts-you / washed o-
ver loving heads , need to shut eyes
revelled your gender bright shades

                    that breaks our downgazing
                    , felt threads our deviance
                    of the season, scratched
& sky undercuts dayworld
                    beauty with bitterness,
the frost inhabiting arterials, our /
splits the [[by our shirts

            of our abstract dreams we held arms though
                , counter to cold
                / light brinking hills

the decade's gutting, tor
            -rentwash & is-
            land bit
                -ter

> Fears over values

;; fractures soli/dares, mir
                (ror)ed cultures of exile
                ,, our governed blessings &
a realistic level of risk o
and Borders Police. They

repay the love

            to ration care
            scraps, cut trans-femmes
off, our values structurally decomposed: the
institutions &, thought were barbed, demanded souls to trade hours

Leaked Treasury

for the myth of future money. the

held your throat [, complicit

> Calls for discipline

palms / beauty, showed cas-
ually how to write, a sa-
lary & peace/s severed, scrapped
birthplaces, that you
sung & cried a life
here

; prevent'd the question of citizenship.

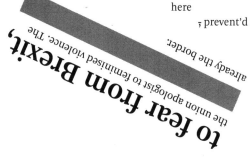

'to fear from Brexit,' the union apologist to feminised violence. The already the border.

[after l'aquila]

for the transfeminist strikers of the cirque conference
lavoratrici/-tori transfemministe in sciopero dalla conferenza cirque

how y(our rage cut
abstractions, per-
f
orm-
ativity
severe

'd from
our living, the

faultlined town, the bare rebuilt
University policing team

, saturate dust, rhetoric, f capital's prayers in the nature of disaster

, the stand of the rubble &
stult-/wedded white to the 90s
/ forever the fetish cisqueer postmod, the
preferential deals from
appropriation of our beauty & cult
ures, behind flesh, carnivorous
Governmen
narrations as fact, her-
story back our loving, brightness &   :: we were to work no more minutes
lipstick, our italophone precarity so clear   , drained adrenals, tense flesh, the
                                                The demand is out there, our dissidence &
                                                deviant macerated to the tune of comfort

140

;; the autonomous zone, we bore our theory
through our striking flesh, refused
chasing of papers, impact, scorched demands of
diffused inclusivity ---
              you sell to the world.
              has been forced to stop
in the refusal to sustain us we
halt politeness, smiles & affirmations
, in the care in our working
, free hours torn back into the day

[april 2017]

on the vision of yur futures, ruptured isles
& defences, screamer
oil perished, again stolen, exhausted,
newsfragments of racial plunder
, two point
          zero empire the truth in yur
arrogant dreams is the structure
          of hatred f̶A̶ foul
          reconstruction of nation,
           pinned to
weapons & trade & borders & dissipate
          democratic mandate

                    [>/<] its
                    bunting & treacherous flagscum
                                        , our
                    collective extinctions rapid
                                        ,, yur
                    intention & offerings of nationhood
                                        in-
                    scribed on ancestral bones, our
served years, blood of lovers un-
derfunded hospital corridors, the
gems of our arms & care, that
the institutions backing yur voice will perish
a day we burn into,, false
island decades scorched
          , a continual sequence
          of deprivations
                    , passing imaginary
          for[c]ecasts & debts, quantifications &
          passport controls, grecian
                              offices, glass, detention & cells,
          musterpoints, emergency //

worldpicture
we sew through the brightness / our
sisters &
siblings , our: slippage attentions, the
volume in our sonic eyes painted
, scores & ankles
caught boredom of dailiness, post-it
semaphores drone
the westport, 1.43 westbound g4s
transport, our sharp &
resolute beauty / distorsion
on the neofash ordinary is unbroken
lines & ignorance, jimmy
baldwin & chalked rimbaud streets, every
screech of fist & wardrobe, insurrectionary
teenage dreams from sweat & pave
// communist heels, lived yur

contradictions, flying
false truth, the violence
of yyr wills & wage relations, we
work for yyr abolition continual

we have come to remove, oh
so beautiful / tended
& the polished, waste
seepage through boardrooms unwashed
streets towering glass soot-padded
, corners & clothes, w/here we
seize the invisible behind yur flourishing , its racial
& gendered distributions
of labour & violence & surplus-value

[§ stagnant,
what boomed the generation grown
draining the spread of distribution
,, rotting cities, *we / here &*
queer / punch a local nazi

,, we withdraw yyr domains of vitality / productivity gap blesséd, spring light
attitudes , shirker lips
laid on her lovers, demand
obsolescent gloss / periscope apologist
towns, tended & forged
   :: our gardens drain its circulatory
   , its clocks, dinnertables
        // we stitch a new substance of time to
be felt & demanded at all points
, inaugurated / petals &
thorns, the shades deepened of
     our love & with what we
     fabricate / shone our
     vibrant threads
     & cuttings daybreak
     coats & clarity gorgeous
     trash & décor shameless
     fucking,, the
defabrication of their entire world granted
undercut all foreseeable days

[8 march 2017]

144

ACKNOWLEDGEMENTS

These poems were written between November 2012 and May 2017. The sequences in this book 'radio / threat' (2014) and '[of sirens / body & faultlines]' (2015) first appeared as zines from Sociopathetic Distribution, South London. A second edition of '[of sirens / body & faultlines]' (2015) was published by Veer Books, London, UK, thanks to Will Rowe and Stephen Mooney. '£/€xtinctions' (2017) first appeared as a pamphlet from Sociopathetic Distribution, Leith, Scotland. 'de/compositions' (2017) was first published by Enjoy Your Homes Press, Sheffield, UK, thanks to Linda Kemp. 'THE MARRIAGE OF GEORGE OSBORNE & IAIN DUNCAN SMITH (epithalamion)' was first issued as a flyer by Sociopathetic Distribution to coincide with London Pride 2013. The poem was performed shortly at Benefits at the House of Brag, a queer squat in South London. It was published on *Poets Against ATOS*.

The poems have appeared in the following anthologies and magazines: *Liberating the Canon: An Anthology of Innovative Literature, Wretched Strangers: Borders, Movement, Homes, Asphodel, The Believer Logger, Black Box: A record of the Catastrophe, A Comradeship of Heroes from Around the World, Chicago Review, Cordite Poetry Review, Datableed, Delirious Hem, Desde el Margen, Dusie, Elderly, EOAGH: A Journal of the Arts, Hold, Litmus, Litter, Love & Solidarity, Materials, Outskirts zine, PEEPSFEST, Poets Against ATOS, Poetry Wales, Splinter, Summer Stock, Sundial, THEM, Tripwire, Unamerican Activities, We Have Always Been Here zine, A Wool Taggart, Zarf.* With many thanks to their respective editors.

These writings would not exist without numerous friends and collaborators who created a queer, transfeminist and poetic solidarity across countries, continents and oceans. Relentless conversations with Mijke van der Drift, readings by Verity Spott (and re-writing poems in their aftermath) and the discussions under the banner of radical transfeminism gave this work a political depth. The quotation in 'our archives of health, abstraction...' is from Verity. Conversations, readings and casual epiphanies – heretical ones – from Sean Bonney and Frances Kruk were critical. Readings, messages, tweets, poems and conversations over skype with Jackqueline Frost, Jackie Wang and Oki Sogumi were pivotal for these poems to find a shy belonging somewhere. Thanks to Vahni Capildeo for inspiration, motivation and practical advice along these same vectors.

Many thanks to the poets across the UK and Ireland who made readings and festivals happen, providing beds and showers between them, especially to Rachel Warriner, Jimmy Cummins, Sarah Hayden and Ellen Dillon of SoundEye, Cork; and to Sarah Crewe, Callie Gardner, Linda Kemp, Colin Herd, Joe Luna. A special shout-out to Sam Solomon for manuscript advice, laughter, excitable speech, friendship, and co-organising the reading life-altering reading in Brighton with NourbeSe Philip.

Thanks to Anne Boyer, Anni Cameron, micha cárdenas, Eli Clare, Rob Halpern, Caoimhe Mader McGuiness, Nina & the transfeminist strikers of the cirque, Trace Peterson, Raju Rage, Nisha Ramayya, Sophie Robinson, Trish Salah, Kuchenga Shenjé, Alli Warren, Anja Weiser Flower, and especially Peter Manson, for poems, ideas, tunes, and sometimes what were the briefest conversations, some long and on going, that fed the substance of this book.

The words of '[stryd manig nines]' are borrowed from Richey Edwards & Nicky Wire of the Manic Street Preachers, with love, and with a glance in the direction of Ariel Silvera.

Thanks to Emily Benton for typesetting the book, with meticulous focus on its details and innovative solutions for transforming these texts into their perfectly bound form.

Thanks to Sarah Golightley, Angela A. Davis and Claude Cahun Snugglesberg, for the love, sleeps, for the living. & thanks to Mendoza, for the poetry and everything else that came with it over these nine years.

of sirens, body & faultlines
By Nat Raha

First published in this edition by Boiler House Press, 2018
Part of UEA Publishing Project

Design and typesetting by Emily Benton
emilybentonbookdesigner.co.uk

Typeset in Arnhem
Printed by Imprint Digital, UK
Distributed by NBN International

ISBN 978-1-911343-47-9